Wake Me with a Shout
Barbara Summerhawk

Layout and design: Marcellus Nealy
Cover art: Billie Miracle
Cover design: Marcellus Nealy

Tokyo Poetry Journal Publications
Printed Matter Press

Editorial address:
Tokyo Poetry Journal, c/o Jeffrey Johnson
English Department, Daito Bunka University
Iwadono 560 Higashimatsuyama-shi
Saitama-ken 355-8501 Japan

First edition
Printed and bound in Japan

ISBN: 978-1-957704-08-1

Table of Contents

Introduction

Former lawyer—defender of native North American and women's rights—Barbara's got major clitzpah. With forty-five years of life in Japan under her belt, she has distinguished herself in many areas: a 7th dan martial artist "with a slightly aggravating tendency to preen"; Aikido shihan; paragliding pilot; founder of groups such as the Engaged Pedagogy Association, Gender Awareness in Language Education; creator of journals like *Tokyo Poetry Journal*; cowriter of sexual harassment policies at universities in Japan; poet, translator, calligrapher, and retired professor; and student of the Okinawan 3-stringed instrument sanshin. To say that she is a one-person shaker and mover, of plural renaissances, is not an exaggeration. She is not one of those self-aggrandizing ones or career-poet types. She is uninterested in appearing hip. She is modest—but once she graces the stage, there is this figure so charismatic and undeniable. A member of the LGBTQ movement and a pioneer between that movement and literature in Japan, you might get the impression that Barbara would be somewhat pedantic / didactic, but remarkably, her body of poetry is highly accessible, engaging, and dare I write, often entertaining:

free sex peeks for slimy pervs
tricky dicks flashing the fake news we might be
freed from a more frigid future
who wants to wax furniture forever?
(from #Beats me)

Alliteration anyone? Barbara is a Beat, a rapper; when she rolls, she flows like a rhythmic rollercoaster. It is all as unforced and natural as the river rolling in her Tokyo neighborhood. She has graced a plethora of journals in Japan with her poetry—*Abiko Literary Quarterly*, *Printed Matter*, and *Koe*, to name just a few. Her two specially edited volumes of *Tokyo Poetry Journal*—one on Japanese women in poetry and the other on LGBTQ themes—have contributed to balancing the female-male ratio of published pages of poetry, and her launch party for the latter was arguably one of TPJ's best attended event so far. Not to mention that she shone an urgently needed spotlight on the Japanese poetic underground.

Barbara has a rich set of unique experiences in the Japanese poetry world. Shiraishi Kazuko once quoted one of her poems in her work. She witnessed a very drunk Yoshihara Sachiko get out of a car to attend one of the communal workshops in Tokyo many years ago. She also experienced the family member of a lesbian poet attempting to block the publication of that poet's work in **Sparkling Rain**, an early queer anthology of Japanese literature that she edited (which received well-earned praise from a Donald Richie review).

Like Nanao Sakaki, Barbara's poetry utilizes counter-intuitive vehicles to wax poetic in forms such as science and numbers, which are seldom associated with this genre. Edith Shiffert, a poet who also lived in Japan for a long time, wrote often of the simple, quiet tranquility of nature. Barbara's poesie too is marked by praise of Gaia, but it is more interactive, engaged, and playful, as in A River Between Us:

> *we stand together against only*
> *white-hot heat of an Oregon summer.*
> *We speak in tongues,*
> *parables, parabolas of our sacred waters.*
> *Rocks, all rainbow under the clear*
> *sparkling connections we share here*
> *of the cool needs of all our communities:*
> *our fish, our hawks and doves*
> *our weeping willows and our laughing children*
> *our saints and sinners wading,*
> *shouting touching the surface of all our lives*
> *splashed across from one side to the other*
> *just skimming enough to toast this valley*

This is a poetry focused on humanity with the backdrop of nature.

Barbara's poetry covers a wide range of subjects, including

the law and politics (On Hearing that the Oregon Supreme Court Holds the Ban on Gay Marriage Unconstitutional), technology (What Would We Do if We Could), family and friends (Breakfast in Bristol), gender (You, or The Sis Boom Bah of Gender) literature (Disconnect), (Translator's Dream), (The Things We Read on Trains), language (Dear Future), (Antonym), (I Live in Parentheses), and nature and cats (The Comings and Goings of Cats and Other Sentient Beings). Her work even delves into the Japanese avant-garde, as showcased in her writing on Ankoku Butoh, the postwar Japanese form of dance "Butoh Blues," for Hijikata Tatsumi, and on Fluxus poetic forms, collaborating with Yoko Ono's first husband, Ichiyanagi Toshi, and Ay-o. Some poems pivot on a pun and shoot off in unexpected directions. There are also many philosophical dives where a seemingly trivial thought (in this case, an afterthought) turns into a flight of fancy, as in "I Live in Parentheses," a meditation on writing and loneliness:

An afterthought to some main clause.
It's quiet inside the brackets …
There's no subject I seem to relate to …
I'm alone inside these ( )
I don't even know what I modify or if I'm modified;
Who reads me?
People often skip over brackets;
they contain no important or useful information,
soon to be deleted
no name no subject no sense tense
here inside these ({ }), no access to an eraser
let alone a pen.

This interplay between language and thought is highly pleasing, contrasting with the narrator's feeling of isolation. Perhaps sometimes the afterthought can be more telling than the "main idea". People are often put into boxes and labeled, but to be placed in brackets seems like torture, almost like a straight-jacket. What's worse is when the writer has no writing utensil, thus relegating her to futility; we've all been there. These jumps from punctuation and grammar to the literal and then the proverbial appeal to us as lovers of the written word.

This collection spans work penned at least as early as 1967 to the most recent work written in December 2023. The poetry herein can be appealing, playful, and joyous, but there are also serious offerings, such as "There Must Have Been Beaches Near Dachau." In my view, taken all together, there is no more powerful foreign poet in Japan than Barbara. Her work makes me think of all those American Beats, whose wives cooked for their friends when they came over—the work here stands for the antithesis of situations like that. How about those hubby Beats get in the kitchen and then let's negotiate who cooks first every other day. In a fair world, the author of this book would receive an award for being such a formidable poet, translator, editor, and catalyst for literature in Japan and beyond. Instead of the emperor's Order of Culture, let us call it The Bodhisattva's Boom Boom, or The Shakyamuni Shaker Prize. So, as Barbara herself writes (punning on "capital"), hopefully this book will lead to:

coming soon: Barbara in Bantu or Bengali,
my name in capitals around the world
my next sentence my very own.

Taylor Mignon, January 29, 2024

Wake Me with a Shout

#Beats me

Modern Howl
shrieking out from unread, misread
misappropriated texts on
pried open thighs
boobie sketches slyly hitching up our skirts
free sex peeks for slimy pervs
tricky dicks flashing the fake news we might be
freed from a more frigid future
who wants to wax furniture forever?

Hot wax off the hair
the rough places shall be made smooth so to be
run over by that Wild West steamy roller lust
not love never love
remarkable in all of the meta-spores spewed
out across the smoky back rooms of our boredom.

Today, we have hash tags where we once had hash pipes, ha!
Pixelating the perfect image of the beat and brightest.
lashed, then, now
hardly ever at the mic
rarely seen or heard, we stand by
while straight or gay out of Compton
strut, stroke, smash, smite, God, yes, smite
Still
now, us, your lovers, bitches, chicks, cunts, hags, daffy dumb
ditsy damn, yeah
thumbs on the trigger, baby
#Me, too
shit you bet

We Exist

The scientists say, because stars explode
The universe stepped back and said
Nova, baby, blow!
So let's not hesitate
We can all cross-pollinate
new worlds we'll create
& fill with souls that resonate.
Hip hop over to my side of the Tokyo galaxy
where sown by the stars
we sift down, crop up, stand out
we are seeds of faith, seeds of hope
seeds of love and fun strewn across this landscape
Here, now.
Born in a supernova, us
So let's all sparkle like the stardust we are
Shine on!

Unraveling Richard
(For Richard Holbrooke)

Better a peacemaker come undone than the

peace. If you had a cosmic choice to surrender

your sanity to stop a slaughter wouldn't you

sign on? If something is required to be lost

perhaps it is the bite-sized chunks of dignity

dogs of war demand.

Everyone attacked you, you explain nobody

wins, but nobody loses either there was never a

contest where you send in your box-top hopes

the grand prize — a Chevy Nova that explodes

on contact, nothing without a price. You're

an American Ambassador of the laid-back &

laid, America the Babbitful who was striding

across borders looking for Ginsberg's angry

fix? You must have had multiple personalities,

be bipolar, a touch of paranoia wouldn't have

hurt. You sailed to Catatonia learned to beg

for scraps of time and left behind who you were for all of us who couldn't understand that patchwork world that stitch by stitch, peace by peace, could give us the greatest sum of all our possibilities.

On Hearing that the Oregon Supreme Court Holds the Ban on Gay Marriage Unconstitutional

We are all of us free now to choose an aisle

seat for ancient rites

& designer vows; sacred ceremonies to all our

known and unknown

gods, embracing all our eternities, when we

can turn to the people

we love & say "I do baby, I do…" public, out

for all to see; love

trumps fear in the highest courts of our land.

At last we can stand

for it at the altar of acceptance. My mottled old

skin sags into a smile.

At last, at last, free at last, married myself, free

at last.

A River Between Us

I like this
wild river between
us, this green
peaceful flow
around all our diversities
no special
inlets for anyone
we stand together against only
white-hot heat of an Oregon summer.
We speak in tongues,
parables, parabolas of our sacred waters.
Rocks, all rainbow under the clear
sparkling connections we share here
of the cool needs of all our communities:
our fish, our hawks and doves
our weeping willows and our laughing children
our saints and sinners wading,
shouting touching the surface of all our lives
splashed across from one side to the other
just skimming enough to toast this valley
sun setting, the promise of stars
and once again, dawn, always dawn
down on the banks of our
river between us.

Walking to Woody's
For Jonathan

Strapping on the steel teeth of the snowshoes
Can take us striding across the deep, soft
Snow job, slippery slope of a
Gendered discussion on why
Nature creates a seemingly
Bipolar slant on just what it means to be
Human.
You, me
Opposite sides of the same coin
God flips for the fun of it,
Sees if we're up to the walk through a whiteout.
For a time, there on the path we shared,
Only a small blue sign post
Reminds us there is direction to our lives.
We will at some point up ahead
Rediscover the promise of Family....
Uncertain, invisible, yet we plod on with faith that
There will be clarity, one step at a time.
Looming through the fog of doubt
We spot the ski lift, and beyond
A warm fire in a book-laden lodge
We sip coffee to a soft jazz in the background,
Blizzard through the window, opening on a safer view of a
storm.
Woody's, the lodge named for Woody of Toy Story?
The faithful friend tale we can tell to the kids;
We believe–we know
Frost's path less taken;
We beat the crowd, and for a time,
We walked together.

Maiden, Woman, Crone...

I'm up the trail here looking back and
stretching out my hand across the strata
separating our ages. I'm here lifting you up,

the you that was me. Come, I have some
secrets to tell you how to thread the needle
that can sew up the gap in our lives.

You are so young and cynical and so empty of
nice things to say about yourself. You try to,
but don't believe; I do.

I'm here to help you cross the minefield of
maturity. Somewhere up ahead I know there's
another me smiling,

reaching out her hand linking all of us, all the
"me's" inside waiting to tell us about all the
new forms we'll take,

the new ways we'll create together with
nothing more to prove. She is whispering a
word I whisper to you, come.

Dear Future,

I've always loved you, loving your promises

hidden between the lines of my face

laying down with you in the pastures of my past

parchment covering our private parts.

We embrace passionately

you stroke my longings

for a future perfect tense.

Hiding out in the Here and Now

shoving our cushions aside

I want some assurance you'll be there for me

& all my fractal worlds.

We can vow at the altar to accept

our mortal truth but our world

sometimes seems a run-on sentence.

Being shouted from the four corners of the earth

abiding, turning slaphappy inhaling all that carbon

coughing clearing the Amazons out of the treehouses
of our angst and ennui from dusk til dawn.

Streaks across the west are burning
tie your shoes & get to work with this woman
allow all our links to be bug-free
& fill us all with Serenity.

The logo of my letterhead begs that promise
I look forward to meeting you again
I'm back on the bus.

Antonym

A persistent rant we hear today is an anthology

of old-fashioned antidisestablishmentarianism

in the current fantasy of philanthropic giving

to the antithesis of what it means to be an americant

we need to return to a more pleasant

Less antiseptic lifestyle consistant with commandmants

to save our nantural environmant....

Tree Ring Circus

Ring 1

Madrone barks back at seal imposters.

Ring 2

Wise willow says

"Not taking this lion down"

Ring 3

Behemoth performer pines for peace

packs trunk, heads for the Sisikiyous...

Butoh Blues, for Hijikata Tatsumi

You twist fragments of stories
around your body where they
hang
on a twinge of a scream or smile; same muscles used.
Come be an explorer, join in the horror
of what we're never quite sure (being never quite...)
The white mask moves with you as we hide in the crevices
the contortions possible in the disjointed
slow dance on the killing ground.
Wiped out, sighs and sounds arise
Fall
Live and die on a stage
wrapped tightly around our most profound
Poppycocking sludge of a slipstream
nightmare of fears
yet the eloquence of it all may be worth it
Save the last dance for me.

Narita to Me

Wild walk through the Xenophobic maze of
misapprehensions
ironed out, flatlined any hope of remaining off the grid(dle)
Fone, forced into my dinosaur hands to track where I would
be
me alone in the neighborhood of impatience
how do you dial up some fun, hon?
Text try:
No I don't have any symptoms you motherfuckers.
Masked, all, waiting for results
two besties scrape me off the exit door of the airport
& drive me mad(ly) to bed.
This city, Kiyose, shut up, closed down, musing on malaise...
Old crumbs on the floor
feeding the Kafka cockroach
crawling across my kitchen, but mine
refugee from American macho misogyny
I just wanna be free in Kiyose city
I wanna be free, free, me

COLLABORATION: Ichiyanagi Toshi with Summerhawk

Rainbow No. 2 for Orchestra

A totally inexperienced orchestra plays a 7 not major scale on various instruments.

(Ay-O)

Arkestra in Living Color, Beat

Rrrreeed or yelllllo grrrr blue indig ovio uvvvvvvv

7 77 777777777 7 7 7

✤

Ichiyanagi with Summerhawk

Music for Piano No. 5, Fluxvariation

An upright piano is positioned at center stage with its profile toward the audience. The pedal is fixed in a depressed position. A performer, hidden from view in the wings, throws darts into the back of the piano according to the time pattern indicated in the score.

(Ichiyanagi)

Hide, Performer

Hidden dart depresses pedal.

Center stage, piano responds uptight

all right all right

God is in place, finally Mr. Pope.

COLLABORATION: Jeffrey Johnson, Taylor Mignon, Summerhawk

T(aylor)P(arpara)J(effrey) with Reiko

Silent spring night; supermoon rises coughing wheezing in
the breeze
petals fall, bringing down the house of cards
cherry blossom petal blizzard — hold the cliché — ah!
refreshing earthquake peachy keen fever, tulips at a distance,
quivering...
spring steps
a blizzard of quakers in a red dawn
Urawa Lotte chocolate factories, Cedar Rapids Quaker Oats:
Crunch Berries
stocks fall into winter no coins left for laundry; sundried
desert
dateline deadline, headline, where's John Prine?
Lonely tee shirt spins round unlikely bed babes
The Normal Prime Mover Deadheads ineffuckable jam
break out, go viral, dance on my preset grave; atone...
scratch your way out of a premature grave
the coronation and fingers to the bone
1/4 baked geniuses Adderall mad: word-croutons of improv
Caesar

Disconnect

Interbeing, the buzzword among

Thich Nhat Hanh's line

loops us into the greater granola

of our LinkedIn Natural way

yet, yesterday, scattered across

the woven rugs of my residence

were fuzz, feathers, here and there

tiny chunks from the hunt

my cat still racing around with kill in her mouth

spattering the last droplets of the Kingfisher's blood

on the eggshell-colored walls, a new abstract

that celebrates preying as a feline spiritual practice.

She sat on the deck to dine after I ejected her

no mask now, surely purring–

she knows avians are good for her health

the last of the kingfisher crunched

an orange feather on her lips.

It was possibly the same shot of orange and blue

I saw hours earlier along the banks of the Yanase,

an old man taking photos pointing to where it was

he gave me a photo of the bird, electric blue back

      orange breast, long beak we admired

as we watched herons of hope, swallows of serenity....

I might have written a different sort of take

on the world and its ways but

returning home I could sense the sneering

malignant indifference of pain and suffering

that nature can sometimes show us.

If I were a cat, would I enjoy the crunching

on the small bones of our Avian neighbors?

Suppose I might see them there

picking at the last of the persimmons

dangling snacks for my hunger habits?

Breathe in / breathe out

I vacuum up the feathered remains

wondering if someday someone will do the same for mine

when the ultimate stalker catches me napping

I hope so. I prey.

Untitled

At the bottom of a bricked well of worry

stuffed into an amber bottle, invisible
she wandered the neon night
healing lepers and blessing sake machines.

She knew it was the end of the line
the last word on a page
ripped from her mind swimming in the sea of suffering
never washing up on any shore of possibilities,
one foot paused on the train platform...

A man in work boots reaches out his hand
a man who right then dedicated himself
to lifting her from her fallen dreams
Showing her the simple truth in trust
in perpetuity, a man, working in the scaffolding
of the city's shadows; together they learned
to walk sunlit paths gazing at the herons in the river
later, rolling in his chair, he never missed a beat, grateful.

Last Fall, I scattered his ashes on our river,
He flows with the stream
Our lives carved; me, here hopeful
A future received with faith.

I Live in Parentheses

An afterthought to some main clause.
It's quiet inside the brackets
can't see to the end of the sentence
which someone is writing, or wrote
I don't get the tense of things to come from here,
it's like hiding in a hole in a wall
that someone is replastering, but what kind of wall
or who needs it, who designed it
and how the hole got here is not in my light cone.
There's no subject I seem to relate to, nothing that
answers those testy little queries,
I'm alone inside these (   )
I don't even know what I modify or if I'm modified;
Who reads me?
People often skip over brackets;
they contain no important or useful information,
soon to be deleted
no name no subject no sense tense
here inside these ({   }), no access to an eraser
let alone a pen.

Breakfast in Bristol

Whatever magic there was so long ago
in creating life through love (it might've been lust)
is now toast with butter and honey, whole wheat
or chocolate-laced scones covered in fat-free yogurt,
a double dribble of irony there,
crumbs scattered across a tabula rasa
of a new generation,
who know nothing of the rips and rifts
shifting under the feet of the elders not yet doddering
but more cautious of where to step and listen
for the pittering pattering or plodding of folks ahead.
Here
warm kitchen, Karen with coffee in one hand
hugging Samantha, lost in dreams of dance
in and out, with a song, a shout
Mark marches to and fro, the guardian whose shield
still glitters in the sunshine of a child's smile,
off now to an interview, knowing he can return
to the concept of family, safe, anytime.
Kitchen loud, cacophonous, wonderfully so.

When I'm Old

Sitting on some sofa in the Blossom Hill Care Center

what will I remember?
The smiles of moonbeam friends
or Lego monsters I built with my grandson
in loose moments away from those
passionate pink dreams of Barrie's
that could wield words and wands?

Will anyone come when I call
for a change or do I sit quietly aware
of time's inexorable flow
down the hill, past the dump, on its way
to another shore where mad hatters
& pied pipers would listen as we
talked over tea, or dance away with the rats
who at least have a community of something, what was it?
The afternoon fades; I wish to read a story, to have a story
read to me
By whomever stops by this sofa.

Sniper

Shot
from the sniper's point of view
a boy, a woman
armed with an American kind
of desire to decide
run towards a tank full of good ol' guys
tattooed with lacy tracer fire...

We are to believe
this dusty slaughter of mother and son serves us
it guarantees our ski resorts, two-car garages
sepia stills of families that glow in the dark.

When movies matter most
spinning myths for our adoration
informing our notions of heroism,
whether in HD, or on Blue-Ray
2-or 3-D
black and white, or red white and blue livid color
the world is facing us across
lines of coiled wire.

Translator's Dream

Shadows on the cave wall
these translations
can I ever stand in the sunlight
of my own creations?

To live as secondary, an afterthought
observing, writing in someone else's passive voice
putting out page after page of crafted characters
who will live on in the collective literary world
[(translated by:) only in small letters in parentheses]
beastly brackets who brand me inferior partner in all this.

Ah, if only I could not render writing in some other's
language
but my immortal, wise prose: to be translated, to be
announced
coming soon: Barbara in Bantu or Bengali,
my name in capitals around the world
my next sentence my very own.

Small Flakes

White ash blows across the redwood deck
a fire somewhere, far? Not so far?
No hot coals or embers, just the dead white
memory of a tree, was it a fir or pine?

Skittering past my bare feet
Standing here on planks of sawn plans
for retirement, rocking on the backs
of these redwood planks
the ashes still blowing about scattering
our wild forest hopes to the evening winds.

Perhaps the sky will soon clear and here
we'll see deep into the night
the Milky Way, the starry soul
of our universal understanding
past bare feet standing on an age-old deck
sailing on.

Paragliding Memory

Just when I realize I can be as big as my dreams
fly cross country and land on my feet
the meadow of memory calls back the day I left you
cuts me back down to size
leaving me bleeding in the weeds
along the road less travelled.

My friends gathered again to celebrate
our long flights of fancy; it's a beginning
soft chatter in the twilight suggests regeneration
still you're half a world away
angry at the things you've never said to me.

We've flown off in different directions
but weight-shift the harnesses in which we sit
we can turn, land in the same field
walk towards each other, can't we?
Here, here is my outstretched hand...

Right up Behind Him

A cloudy day, no shadows, no feeling of being followed
death hovered a while, no doubt with grim glee
seeing his fading aura in the twilight of a good life, lived.

My friend doesn't turn back
he finishes the shopping plans for the evening
he knows (somewhere in the back of his mind)
his past is rolling up behind him
to the last moment
when he will nod off after dinner, in his chair
he can only have for a time
it's on loan and no one escapes the Final Forfeiture.
I see it coming, I say goodbye again
"See you tomorrow" but tomorrow exists
as a proposition not proved.

In the morning, I will call him, and if he doesn't answer
I will sit for a few moments and recall
all we did, all he gave me, all I wished for him
and not turn back.

My Anger

Dusted across the crescent moon
just before it set behind the pines
teeth on the far side of the ridge
consuming the stars, a well.

A warm, Fall day, the leaves
shocked into gold by an early frost
hasn't cooled the resentment
does the moon have mood, too?
Do the trees regret the dying of Summer?

If I am able to purge these remains
these dregs of last year's lame excuses
will I be promised a Spring?
If I am my only sun can I shine on through?
My self-made anger does not become me
there's no sense in being pissed off at Emptiness.

Should I expect thank you notes
for gifts given with no expectations?

This is how I feel my life sometimes is:
carefully constructed of random paradoxes
oxymorons, dead ends and lost leader ads.

Not that no one is not thankful for my clumsy attempts
at celebrating with, for ...whatever
I never seem to know
it's like being a Protestant standing alone before God
never quite sure God forgives Sin
which I surely have many; better to be Catholic
Set rituals, sacraments, steps to Exoneration--

Act of contrition and I knew I would at least get Purgatory
The bargain basement of religions, but there was certainty.
With you, I never know either whether you've forgiven me.
All these check-in calls, visits, trips I enjoy
but are they gaining me any merit?
Will I die in a state of Grace?
The sacraments of birthday cards
Novenas offered on Instagram
I have to decide if I've finally left Hell
For better digs...

You, or The Sis Boom Bah of Gender

I've searched   through the ruins of
my dreams   of belonging, of
family gatherings   in the sunrise of
communities settling on the prairies of
          our platitudes

No flatscreen time, only flatlined screams
tapering off with hollow whimpers.

We had to turn around what
it means of
who we are embed with
we go dingbat for

Who wraps us in rainbows, no matter.
our new families celebrate self-same love
freeing the sis boom bah of gender
no more nixed rolls in the hay; we own the barn, babe.
Let me touch you lick you
tickle you love you by all means
let me, set me, vet me, forget me, let me
free,
you.

Something's Up

I never knew how much
the Milky Way meant to me
then the smoke from the fires move in
& we were left with Vega
only Vega at the top of the sky
peeking through a thinner layer of purgatory
must be like this
no stars, a faint blood-red moon
in a grey blah that blurs
our memories of other summers.

Other fires burn our sins of complacency
to a red hot glow & send these days
of severe limits on our plans
for the merest of pleasures below.

If we had been more passionate, more loving
would the lightning have struck somewhere else?
Is this our random fate for a life lived half awake?
Surely the Milky Way is up, there
waiting for a more transparent series of nights
where we can retire to a grassy field
after a virtuous day in the Garden.

Adam and Eve, hand in hand
still had the galaxy even after the Fall
god couldn't be that mean.
It's up there, tracing its glow all the way
to the end of my horizon and beyond
I have to believe that smoke clears.

Trucks

Shoot out from the corner of my eye
taillight so swallowed in the morning mist
leaving me behind
shaking in the wake
of the possibility of becoming
a one-dimensional smear;
such power roaring by
my pitiful attempt at 50 cc.
Yet later at the next stoplight
I streak by the stackup of all those
Semi snobs
I get to my goal at my own speed
with no load to carry.

Shifty Gears

My old Toyota truck
seems to be slipping
gears go in and out
causing me to clutch
for stasis: a state of no change
where it's always sunny, streams full of fish
riverbanks of serenity, and friends forever
throwing pot lucks.
Everyone shines on
harvest moons
Singing karaoke & no one talks of
change
small, or exact or otherwise
as inevitable, to be embraced.
The only moment I want to
hug
to my heart is this one, this one
this happy heckofa moment
no change, please.

What Would We Do if We Could

Ascend the power lines
and assume some god hood?
Redirect the traffic with omnipotent apps?
Stem typhoons and level
       the playing field just so?
Would it help if all boys and girls
dropped the centerfield fly
losing the game for the team?
Would rewriting our pasts to make all women
good wives, wise mothers
end the Meiji Period sooner?
Write poetry that needs no editing?
Woulda...

Raw

Migrates across continents
settles into the new soil
sifts down into incomplete
cracks and crevices
sending out shoots of
half-baked hopes that grew
through the summer
penetrating deep into stew
of our simmering concerns
twisting & stirring quiche
quests for taste
wondering how to hype the whole
slowly fading into our parade, proud.
Cooked
rolled, diced, then spliced
into the menus
boasted, broasted, fried

Stars Pelt Russia
(2014 meteor shower hits Russian city)

Dear god,

I understand you don't monitor every meteor
still a whole universe out there
and you managed to dump a load
of rocks on a hapless hamlet?
If this all started with a Big Bang
it may end in a Big Whimper
as pebbles fall, no apologies rain down
no, "Oops, sorry, wrong planet"
just gravel strafe the unaware.
If you had hit the USA,
would the NRA have put out a call
to machine gun the godless?
If we don't believe in you, or don't want to
are we doomed to a world with no consequence?
We can't even mount a campaign for recall
or march against the violence we suffer
there's no malice in an indifferent universe
where do deities takes the fall, or even cops to creation.
Is the world not turning out the way you wanted
so you're in a snit and pepper somewhere with pebbles?
You could push erase; we'd never know.
Better maybe for us than burning up or fading into the dark?
Is there an answer? I'm scared of today's ring tone.

Our Images of Free Flight

Holden Caulfield, Thelma & Louise
drive over cliffs we jump from
our first brief flutters, a taste of wild skies
can sink us so fast down to earth for a hard
look at our self-concepts, inadequate to handle
what we need to do, finding ourselves
tossed around, jacked up to cloud base &
dropped into alfalfa fields, calling for a retrieve &
drive back to top launch.

Free talking, armed to the teeth with Truth
there's no telling how far we can go
one step on a windy day
back up, rising strolling
in the canyons of clouds
leaving our obedient forms behind
into the pure blue, always above us.

Work in the Fields

The fresh clean
rain
at dawn--
brush strokes against my cheeks
cool blush in the silent walk
to the fields.

Burnt blush dripping
salty rain in my eyes
mist the distant line
of palms frozen
in the heat.

The truck paces
our hearts as we gag
on berries ripe
for the bakery pies.

On through the day
the sun, the brassy air
beats us down
to one color.

Boiling surges flush
my brain lifting crates.

Clean for the dawn
we lie with eyes opened
waiting for the cool blush
of love and power
as our sweat flows into the earth
together, pure.

If I Had My Way

1.
I have always walked hot dusty roads
with blood on my hands
searching for a drink.

Even at my calmest, clear blue sky blessing me
storms rage icy winds blow thru my illusions

Raped, raped, raped again
you, for a semen rush
crushed another sister
under your tread
man of the house
you probably wore stud
bell bottom jeans
or the late great
square-toed shoes &
you were so cool.
You came out of movies
trying to sneer like Brando
walk like Newman
screw like Superfly.
All lies, but you bought every one
whether you're 20 or 50
limp dick or power piston, baby you're it

2.
So casually here on the road to the lake
I see sleek strong bodies
trunks covering their only claim to power &
again I dream of blood
seas of blood, your blood
washing us free

I'd take you & suck out all the filth & leave you all
Hollow Men standing there on the Wasteland
wine dark seas from Homer suggest
purifying waves I'd swim in, carrying me to a new world.

You smashed her face on this road
strands of blond hair clinging to the rock you used
every one of you is a rapist
god, for a machine gun, but that would be too fast.
Castrating bitch? Of course!
I want to step out on a pure spring morning
sun surging thru my veins, no longer spiked
by nightmares of monsters
swaggering across masses of sagging flesh
propped up for false promises
stand up & face the dawn with a knife
glinting in my hand, strong, ready
I'll spring on you & slice off your balls &
without balls, you'll no longer exist
you couldn't laugh or cry or play or work or survive
you'd go off to watch bullfights &
write great novels about life—
more rapes, prick ripping in thru battered thighs
long live anarcho syndicalism, Jesus Christ, &
Kaiser Wilhelm (Reich Guard)

3.
Even diving into the cool water
I think of shores littered with your limbs
ah, the swift act of raising an axe &
smashing all your faces
the blade slicing you open neatly
blood soaking into the sand
with the sun beating down on my back

one act of purity
no kiss ass or kick ass
one pure act

You write books on us, music, you make
pudding of our dreams & matchsticks of our arms
you keep us from loving each other
from the furnaces that would cast us
in steel molds together

You talk all the time
" teach classes and run the coops
" take over & tell us with your eyes
where we belong -- down under.
Come around again brothers
oh no, what do I want?
Off yourselves or stand there
while I raise the axe.

4.
A breaking of the day
a pause before noon
hot dusty road &
I'll kill you, cut out your heart to feed my cats, &
maybe at dusk,
I will return to bury you
bleed into the earth
apologize for now.
At my leisure, I will decide, once & for all

I will decide.

J. Alfred Prufrock and the New Feminism

Prufrock, your creator
was born with silver hair &

your world is the Madhatter's tea party
with China cups & silver spoons
it grows old, it grows old
we won't do what we're told anymore

The half-deserted streets call us
to come dance and meet face to face
leave your coffee spoons
stainless still metronomes
measuring out your life in daily schedules
no time for indecisions & revisions
rip off your collar & let your head turn free.
We must disturb the universe.

Together, all of us we'll let the voices
out of the farther room
& chase the yellow fog back to the sea.

Tip the footman for the last time
it's your decision
I mean, I really mean
forget your wrinkles.

Presume, roll up your trousers &
ask the Mermaids to sing to you.
Hand in hand walk in the cool surf at ebb tide.

The end of your world is the beginning of ours.

Jets

Taint the sky with threats of the stone age.
We swim in the pure green water
defined by ragged limestone walls
cooling our flesh
watching the clouds of bubbles
rise around our bodies, rise toward the sky.
Cool drops of rain fall from our hair
onto the burning, naked rocks as we climb
past the NO TRESPASSING sign
hooked to a strand of barbed wire.
The Sheriff ready to enforce his frustration
"Let's go. This is it, the last time."
Steve turned to him and said
"We're through with all that,"
And we all walked past the sign
and the sheriff, on down the hot dusty road
our eyes on the sky
waiting.

Mainlining

Plastic dolls shoot up
on silicone
breasts expand, are grasped
by cold metallic hands
of studs programmed
to cover the needle marks
with cashmere patches.
Strobe lights
surge
aching minds
higher away from horse
infertile stud
that drains minds
as it fills veins
with pastel shades
of fire
and empty hopes
of words
made flesh.

1977

A Confessor of Psychology
famous for his treatise on love
whispered softly
feed the sick
and bury the dead
or was it
feed the dead
and bury the sick?
Softly whispered
the Confessor of Psychology

September 1

Today I bent, folded & mutilated
August
stuck it in my mouth & swallowed it whole.
Coughing up the $s for rent not quite August
caused the friendly acquiesance
in pineapple & coconut drinks on the waterfront.
Today a friend sang for the meant for dead &
she cried out for a rope to hang from.
My last dime was spent & I couldn't afford rope
so she went unhanged to the butcher's funeral
while the baker & candlestick maker
stood by, faces in the crowd.
When I asked her why she breathed
a barely audible scream
I changed the subject to object & returned to go.
In a game, in a shadow
there are briefs to be filed
on the Subject & Object.
We played monopoly in prison after the fall
& chess after the appeal
so chase down the rainbow
with a siren you turkey
any violation of the ordinary
deserves a ticket, doesn't it?
I never did learn to tear along
the dotted line.

Tell Harold the Mice are Dead

Harold (an ex-pusher
who spends most of his
life in a bottle),
always cowered
on my rusty springs
      afraid
of the mice casting dice
in the alley behind the stove.

Coexisting is like that, someone sneaking up
& knocking at the back of my heart, none need ask
I've got Old King Cole & all the crows singing
to me & me to them.

Walking on Fisher's old pond one bright sunny day
a waterbug slipped into my blood stream
& told me how to live.

Late at night someone paints
the inside of my forehead orange
waking, I hear the moonlight
laughing down on the corner with the wind.

Oh, they invited me all right, but it's too early to play
I haven't seen a sun rising over the Snack Bar yet.

I went to law school because
(in 25 words or less)
I have law blood sugar &
I need a heart stimulant &
Harold crawled into the mice one night
(to find out where their heads were at, so to speak)
& the last I heard was that he runs around

with a bunch of olives in a Reno discoteque.

Harold knew time better than me
he couldn't shoot up on parking ramps
sometimes it's the smells that creep up
& tickle the hairs on the back of my neck.
Two corpses in the alley gassed or starved
I swept them up & threw them with the others
outside, looking for streets to walk & clocks to set.

I'd wire Harold that Mice Are Dead, but
he wouldn't believe me (& then neither would I).

Close the Courts, It's Christmas

Stars and Bars and Stripes
lash across the backs of people
forced to build ivory towers
for the weak excuse of perfection.
Junkyard dogs express more honesty
than the self-centered serfs of decay
at least they know their lives are built
on garbage and with patient dignity
await their turn to tear out the last shred
of heart from the whole, the whole being greater
than the sum of its hearts
reputation is paramount in the Ivory City.
Grinning healthy masks wrinkle the skin below
Shadowing the hollow souls who never saw the moon.
Silence is expected of all those working in the shops
chunking and shaping the vanilla blocks
sweating in furious dawn they prop up
their strong backs, the paper towers of soft-tongued
and reasonable, by all means reasonable judges.
Sentencing those who shout to rot in pigeonholes
the proper authorities risk their lies
on faded yellow pages and stuff that filth
into the mouths of ones whose minds stirred
once and were silenced once again.

After all, the time passed telling tailors
how to sew and lifers how to live
a degree grants one conditional and summary
power to stop short the breath of the young.
Ann of Archee once whispered
that truth flitted about in late-night forays
into the drugged minds of cleaning ladies.
Tiptoeing no longer, she sings out

her new-found lungs while the shouting, singing
crowd trumpets; pale ivory walls barriers
to the sun crumble at last.
All those who voted to push
around the (Toilers)
Stand trial for treason while ones
who were in contempt of court can
spit on the judge, turn their backs &
Walk quietly, OR LOUDLY
        Over the hill
                and far
                        away.

Dressing to Attend the Funeral

My old Aunt–
90 years of losing light slowly
dressed yesterday in the Home
to attend Cathy's funeral
1933, she died in childbirth
(shabby excuse for why–
we all die a little in childbirth)
& Marion slips on a faded print in the morning
& waits, patiently, for a trip ...
moist soil pounding on our final roof
locks us into what we can be
& Marion sits, wondering why we refuse
to drive her one last step to sisterhood.

After this visit, what can I say?
Forty years from now some hollow smile
will assure the demonstration was cancelled
& they don't need me for theater
if love finds me hiding under the bed
afraid of one more day alone
knowing we have not defeated
one final enemy, will someone drive me
to Cathy's funeral?
Marion will probably need me there.

Epstein's Twice Removed

A cousin of mine once remarked
on the stark nature of Zen monasteries & college towns.
At least the Zen minds wanted to sit & stare at walls
while the campus deans plot the world
in one-inch squares, never integrate
missing the masses of leaves who vote to fall
at noon together, so they may lay in the sun for a while.
Today, the city removed Epstein's for a second time
fulfilling the promise of new parking lots.

A quiet bookstore, where one could find ways:

> to knowledge
> to backyard dreams
> to courthouse scandals
> to poems hiding

> on the bottom shelf.

The first time they ripped apart
the store, we wondered what now?
As the ancient bricks crumbled into dust
we were all one step ahead of the bulldozer
watching the book dust rise into crisp air &
fall back to the worn sidewalk of Clinton Street.
Then the parking lots grew to feed the concrete folks
while sheetrock masked the sounds
of a thousand angry cries, judges called out our orders
while we forced marched, counting footsteps
as we shuffled our opinions into well-made decks.
Earth shoes & records broke out
& the forever cure disappeared
as the sun bounced around & was sedated.

City councils & bad women pow wows
joined hands to state, through loudspeakers
What was next on the program &
What skins were to be mailed to Washington.
"I haven't got very much to store," I said
taking shots of gin off the wall,
& the men in grey coats, I thought they'd be white
whispered softly:
"You've been dead for a long time, come along."
I threw them out with yesterday's garbage
coffee grounds & old bills
walked to the neighborhood park
to reconstruct a few scenes & munch
some stale popcorn buttered with Kent State.
"Why?" I asked the newly feathered sparrow
"Am I appointed guardian for misbegotten dreams
revolutionary tracts, hind legs going weak?"
"Because," he whispered, "The worm never liked
Nicely tailored lawns." That, too, made sense
when I spun on my heels
& made tracks to my door.

From the Flophouse Window

The world twists & writhes
with snakes & lizards
& shaky sounds
of liquid splashing
out of wrists
limp with futility.

In the dark, slowly fading
the dying fires
of a thousand tribes
struggle with the corrupted air.

From the flophouse window
eyes are filmed by bourbon
amber little-ease that cramps
us into Ancient Age
numbs us for our forced march
away from
Grass
     &
         the
             ocean
eternally
     rebelling.

Hitchhiking Law

Catching an early morning song
with an Interstate Thrush flashing past
my blind spot, I wait for my perfect ride
an orange van with quadraphonic sound
full of women headed to Grace and Rubie's.

A truck passes, then 100 ghostly stares
at my patient, humble thumb.
Poems rise to the surface & crack
into harmless chunks to be strewn
alongside the highway debris.

When I finally get to Iowa City
the mist will be burned away
the sun branding the road
in the back of my head as I
walk forward casting no shadows
work & play merge on the Pentacrest.
A frisbee flashes past my blind spot
as I try to write a brief.

Tomorrow, if I have to go to court
at least the early morning mist
will know why
organize the sunshine crew
the cyclone gang must be destroyed.
New worlds
Await the repair of
Our
      dictate
          machine.

The Yellow Brick Road

never really led to an I.B.M. computer. Only a
picket fence in need of paint. Post script: the
highway commission allotted only 7.2% of its
budget for Yellow Brick Road repairs.

Rainbows will now only appear for the
rejected. Charlie, if you're not a Starkist tuna,
Del Monte ain't so bad, but check out the
connection first, don't get stuck with a bad
line. Canning never was my media.

One-dimensional Hound

As the car crushed dog-life into the asphalt
we wondered about appearances.
Walking back meant our acceptance
of the one-dimensional hound.
These days, blood on the highway
raises nobody's eyebrows
we're not even sure whether it was a dog.
Meanwhile the people come and go
worried about sun and ice and snow.
In a more profound future
crushed bodies might give rise
to a new physics new formulas
black holes present themselves
as reminders of the winding down of time
yet no one can escape the stench
of now-dead, sizzling on the Interstate.
Shall we cook dinner?
What of the afternoon swim?
Death stalks our every move
So why show concern that it caught one?
Put your hammer down and cycle away
tear off to the dark side of the circus tent
elephants still sing on strange lands to be seen.
If we shovel the body into light
and clear the road for our homecoming
we have made the leap to feel the rain and sun.
Perhaps tomorrow we can all
Talk without worry
and whistle together a new tale.

Children

A hand-carved Peruvian gourd on my table
grins at the blond freckled boy
with his rubber-frog dreams.
Monica and Gwen stopped to bring me daisies
& I gave them pictures of the Milky Way.

You ask me to lock up my love in your safe
& spare you the shares of my children.
If I loved no one but you
what has the world to gain?

Jason watches Star Trek warping out of orbit
later we skipped down to College Green Park &
learned the theory & practice of Merry-Go-Rounds.

After dinner we play chess & stare at maps
of half-made moons creating crescent shadows
of puppies touring cobblestone streets.

My green-eyed gymnast cartwheels into the kitchen
helping with the almond oatmeal cake
reminding me of last year's shooting stars
that laced across the Colorado sky
lighting our glowing faces.

One more campfire, a run along the ebbtide shore
wet sand printing our story of the day.

If I loved no one but you
how has the world gone on?

The green and gold marching colors of my
youth turn around and around

choosing a new drummer I shall
call to children from the furthest warm beach
promising a new myth, not a computer
print-out on motherhood.
Now the legend joins hands circling, circling
hand in hand we study the quiet collective
with the sparrows, swallows and fronds
starfish in the saltwater pools on coral reefs
postmarked my new appointment:
poet-mother in residence
beneath my skull, and still the children beckon me
as I dance a jig with mop and pail in hand
I softly sing of you, of all of you.
If I loved no one but you
What would we all have learned?

There Must Have Been Beaches Near Dachau

My days have been / are
an old shabby string of rooms
on the edge of Urban Renewal
I crack & fade in filtered yellow air
too long ago, lost on my way to a window...
if I breathe deeply my lungs fill with the rot
of barely audible screams

In the past beaches meant deep green truths
live, sparkling tonic childlike chatter
breaking over all sun unhindered by sinking
grey webs blasting out of the ovens.

Swimming thru the murky green-black waters
I see the Radiant Streams from the Surface
cool confessional washing me clean, absolving
The Holy Ghost always above me
& just out of reach a twinkle in its beady eyes
always learning the cruelest joke:
as I break the surface tension the feeling comes again
punching some Cosmic Time Clock
repeating the same hours

O the cool seconds
I enjoy bubbles swishing my skin
Look at the children
bobbing
      up
           &
                 down!
Dragons of a friendlier age
If a laugh escapes (silly, I always want to
keep the mirth bottled for a later tasting)

it soon dissolves into the air
helping to dissipate the hydrocarbons
then I want to drink the whole sea & sky &
there must have been beaches near Dachau

How will I tell them? They're into water and sun
not the crushing blows of poisoned showers
Once we all awoke finding the blood & strips
of dried flesh emptily sticking to our teeth

We simply went on crash diets hoping we could
macrame & croquet our way to knowledge

Years of struggling with sisterhood
I tried to run from the shadow of my hind legs
There I am again in the string of old rooms
watching parades of skeletons crawling for the alleys
The sun never comes thru pure
I find a job & lose my soul &
cautiously step over women whose sweat
runs off flooded sewers of main street

Excuses, excuses
power plays are caused by hormones
(or the will of God)
Can you explain that to a woman
crawling away from bomb craters?
once in my anger & rage tired of sick yells
gushing out of shaky wrists
macho stomping up & down
goose-stepping fits men so well
I threw a heavy glass & broke a sister's knees...
back I go cracked & faded tearing down ovens
          under a dying sun

They filed down your kneecaps
expecting to make a point of my sins
you won't genuflect to anyone again
perhaps that is part of the Solution
          (or maybe the Problem)
strength can mean taking the truth &
finding a new love from this endless pain.
if that is not possible, if that is not what we can
learn from the beach near the oven
I never swam & all of you
never cast a shadow

There Won't Be Any Trumpets Blowing

In the days of the candy transplant
all this cool talk of dope
never stirs the dust on the back porches
rotting under the freeway
carrying freaks to Disneyland.

Doc Savage flits through the dreams
of soured men curled to protect husks
crumbling in the soft winds
sweeping the city at street level.

Superman and Lois Lane
made a fortune killing flies...

In the bay, cabin cruisers
search for a new fuel.

The Thousand Fires of a Dying Tribe (or Sailing to Catatonia)

COME NOW
Once upon a time was our story line
a kicker for the Better Business Bureau
shadowing us in a '77 eggplant-colored Continental.

Finally, we have reached the organization
we shake hands with Judges who stare
with the confidence of well-made masks.

My jaw no longer drop at folks being gassed
      in the halls of misbegotten dreams.
Pragmatic new ideas break out in a rash
& hide the flush of our faces.

The Ghost Dance chilled rigor mortis
      from setting in too soon.
Moonlight flings only meant morning's distasteful truth.
The fires are ash & so are our mouths.

If we could rake out the coals & spark
a new zestful flame for tea, but our arms are all
matchsticks and our bodies are bound for kindling.

We learn that fodder knows best & that trying, trying
for compassion only results in default judgements.
Protesting was by motion & Catatonia became the isle to
visit.

WHEREAS the plain Jane seeks for the relief
the sum of at least two months of good times
prays that she be granted an injunction to become 3-D

On the hillside the night before
thousands of fires sparked our frontal lobes
with black & white, or color promises of the moment.
Hours passed, we could tell because the sun
peaked through the magic & was gone.

So now the yellow fog creeps in past our office windows
& we blink back the tears we need.
COME NOW the defendants in the cosmic lawsuit
& move the universe be dismissed.

In lieu of the motion being overruled
we will have to wake up & plan chaos better
then send the bill to God

The Waxing Moon

rises from the rippling black waves of the Iowa River
and reminds me that everything is black & white in
the shadows of the pale sky. The sweat cools my skin
rapidly as if my body was the Earth itself. Throwing
back the Infra Red, the heat knowing there's a time
for cool and frosty attitudes. Summer got lost in the
shuffle; aberrations in three-four time replaced the
usual quarry-green afternoon meetings with water
snakes. Query the stars, dull now in the late October
night. Why my heart beats as I run from one point to
another, keeping my center, moving as the earth stirs
the new-laid dust resting at my feet. Pardon the wind,
no one has passed me by to hear my tell-tale heart,
so the rapid pace is my own choosing no act for the
weekend crowd, no tapes to break, no races to run but
my own. Over the river, it runs on into the night and
I, a friend, run on into time.

Where It's At & Where Etc.

Today this cat wants to know where it's at. Eighty years
ago? I don't know, like trying to catch a bullet before it
blows your mind. So I said yeah, man, I might know. Maybe
I could tell you of all the ats of yesterday & all the twisted,
tortured snowflakes melting on a pile of coal. Lumpy stacks
of limbs come branded in the night to feed & clothe a nation
of people minus X. Raped, impaled, roasted, their bones are
cast aside & reassembled beneath the hell-made sun. On the
verandah, the ladies sit in iced-tea comfort: even the distant
screams could not scare them. Lemon-sachet can't keep the
vultures away from the rotting hearts burning on the altar of
some enlightened god. A hundred years in Sinai pursued by
bleached madmen with memories of babies boiled in sweat
wrenched with whips to make the next day's stew, hunting
down their silent screams, on buckling earth in bloodied
dreams of vengeance for rape. They saw themselves commit
& bury the seeds in banquets of slashed-off balls & strips of
smoking flesh.

Up to Utopia, crammed into stony wombs stillborn. On the
street, a man pisses his life away while up the alley, two
cops fuck near a pregnant girl. They just beat to death with
Pepsi Cola -- hits the spot. Page twenty of the evening Times.
Along comes Snow White & the Seven Dwarfs pushing
Woodrow Wilson poppies all ground & set to smoke Up God
Bless America & jet set brings back silk & tea, more hacked
meat for greedy teeth to rip. Babies cry beneath a ton of
shit. Fifty floors below the cocktail party for a minister of
defense who needs more guns but runs for senator instead.
& they pass the hat-bail for that hop-head in the corner who
takes the cash and throws it in the fire, laughs, watching
asses wriggling in the flames for fives, generously given. As
flesh sloughs off from silver bones, he rolls on the floor &

prepares another fix. Somewhere in that night a girl runs, she's fourteen years & loves to tease. Shot brains spatter, the cop pleads self-defense. No one mourns: We're still worn out from Dallas.

The future wears a barbed-wire grin. Distant chatter zings & pops through my illusions. The camps are corning: Their roller coaster's going to jump the track: so let's groove. Pull the pieces together, get stoned, learn the lines tonight, for in the morning silence we'll be cast in steel molds.

New Yarn

Why are all the women quietly knitting in houses
knitting quietly the Big Yawn?
Silently comes the dawn
the dawn, the dawn, the dawn
creeping from the ashen sky
quietly comes the dawn
drifting, sifting
quietly burying women
knitting in houses
knitting quietly the Big Yawn.
snow comes to teach us of warm
naked rooms to be filled by us
forging our needles
riveting, with strong bulging arms
clasping the steel to our breasts
welding and grinning beneath the skein masks
inventing seams we never dreamed would hold
indeed
we are all the women quietly knitting a new Yarn.

The Comings and Goings of Cats
and Other Sentient Beings

Does sentiency depend on seniority?
Is it related to senility?
Surely, we must have a measure for the illusive
consciousness + frivolity = sentiency quotient.
Cats have a high SQ QED.
Cats intuit which door opens on summer
which door to leave closed on dog days
cats come silently shedding
eons of bad karma on my couch
they drape themselves across exits
daring us to take responsibility
for walking out or on.
Cats know robins are good for their digestion.
Cats wish us luck with our pontifical moonlight strolls.
Cats love hunting in the early morning dew
for gophers to grace my breakfast table.
They purr the mysteries, the pity
of our being reborn humans.
They dominate carpets and submit to soft brushings
they are sentient beings who welcome us
Home
every cosmic afternoon.

Three Quarrels

It had to be done
stopping the fight between two grade school boys
on the sidewalk slugging it out over a botched joke
a tackle, we pulled into a driveway, slogging
back to the boys, muddy, punching it out in the rain.
A third boy stood aside, pleading

"We're all friends, okay?" it wasn't
I could see the futures of these three -
the overly sensitive artist who can't take a joke
the blind critic of difference
astounded that anyone could get that angry at him
the perfect pitcher and the ineffectual peacemaker
wondering what went wrong and if it was his fault anyway...

Then there were the two of us interlopers
interested in ending this fight, all fights
self-consciously pleased at our choice of interference.
Once the boys were on their separate ways
we, too, returned to our argument
ahh, no our discussion on a matter of principle
I don't remember, perhaps
it was on the nature of men and boys roaming
freely, entitled to everything we're not
all I have left from that day is a sense of outrage
we've been tricked into fighting each other
and mediating male spats
yet we do encourage the boys
to shake and make up
they never will. The tears will dry
but the tracks on all our faces remain.

Muggers

Today I confiscated those little mug shots
my students knock off
Linking them together
in a solid bloc I can't enter

                                                   &

cut them to ribbons
wrapped the confetti of my
                failure to communicate
into a slash and burn package
for my Christmas holidays.
I want them to worship me
                at the altar of interest
God, she's great, she's so entertaining
something like that
after class I give them back
their fifteen seconds of fame
                in the photo booth.

Passes

I was born in the middle of a bypass
or at least that's what my house became
concrete reality that pushes people like me
onto the off ramp, permanently
our lives become a series of passes!
Underpasses, lateral passes, bad passes
a series of Rites of Passes
to another universe that doesn't have this
whiz bang bargain basement sale
        of a whirled world
it's there, full of twisty little lanes
off the beaten track
waiting for someone like me
to ground break the magnificent.

A Time for Treason

Just now, a moment's scrap of peace
thrown on to us to nibble
while they lace up their Jackboots
turn elsewhere ready to trample
someone else's sacred ground.

Ripping up sanctuaries roasting doves
burning books, these are our leaders.

Do we need to crash into the White House
can we stop this global Götterdämmerung?

We have awakened to find we are not gods
we are not alone and we are not at peace.

A new century beckons before us but we're caught
between a holocaust and a promise of stars
still at Ground Zero, frozen in the headlamps of history.
Daisy-cutting our way into world consciousness
every bit as bad as bin Laden.

Our decades of death squads surely don't call
for the crushing of innocent lives
but the new questions are still the old ones:
Who is innocent?
Who deserves to die?
Who judges?

Ah, the choice of which soda to sip
or which SUV can get us to the mall faster
this is what we pledged allegiance to.

Our stars and stripes fly forever over
the golden arches and G.I. Joes.

The Most Important Question for Us:

How to get through the middle of next Tuesday.

Monday tripped and fell into Tuesday
which crashed and burned Wednesday
went down without a survivor.
Thursday opened with promise
then wondered off on its own.
Friday fizzled on the second light.
Even Saturday whined its way into Sunday
slipping, sliding across to this
      Weak end.

Long Distance

I really have no thing to say to you
about who I am or who I think you are
& never who we could be.
If I could set us free from this
mother-daughter thing lurking in the shadows
of the kitchen or the laundry room
only you tend then we might hang out
our dirty laundry & come clean.
That is maybe asking too much at the moment.
Leave it at annual visits to the grandkids
& occasional beach haven & a game of Risk
long distance, always long distance
the charges never get any cheaper.

The Things We Read on Trains

Cell phone ads
Beer labels stuck to the seat in front
Mystery novels with happy endings
Essays about strong women and nerdy men
       who marry, quarrel , divorce, remarry
       only to find daughters
       who relate to reality TV
Japanese for busy adults
Japanese for the mentally challenged
Japanese in 30 days
Why we don't have to study Japanese
       the Japanese-English grammar
Cheat sheets
Cliff Notes on
       Huckleberry Finn
       The Iliad
       All of Proust
       Yu Miri's novels
Primers on Yu Miri
Watch-band engravings
Tie-pin kanji
Emergency door opener instructions
Map of the subway
Juice commercials
Caution! Something Sexy
School come-ons
Designer clothes logos
Tattoos
Courtesy seat requests
Hanging soft core porn fliers for tabloids
Announcements about the next station.

What Was It I Said?

Was it something heretical to some ancient deity
who hoards knowledge and power
jealously; our potential for compassion
our awesome capacity for love?

On the physical plane
we have our limits, we do
Larry died; life's limit reached
the very edge, then, razor thin
our margin of error or the indifferent universe
sneering at our attempts at grandeur.
Well.
It was a life lived with love
and to his last limited breath
he was a starburst of a brother.

Barbed Memories

In Spring, the water level in the lake
drops a little, it is, after all, a reservoir
irrigating and placating Western Tokyo's cabbage patches
giving way to condos rising steadily towards city center.

Walking this shore again, I see the barbed wire
remnants of a fence that had set neighbors apart
keeping one's livestock to oneself.
Old, old fence posts exposed
and rusting twists of iron
dulled by decades of dips in the drink.
In its day, they could rip and tear
surely these barbs left ragged wounds
that slowly healed into thick scars
rough, ribbed reminders of the limits set by
some anonymous, arbitrary force.

Here, now, the once-sharp wire tickles my bare feet
        no longer capable of causing pain.
Seasons pass and our former fences that hemmed in our youth
with pricks and stabs of abuse lie dissolving
in the calmest of ponds warming, waiting.

So Trapped in the Youth Game After All

My friends dye their hair or buy expensive wrinkle-removing
creams
that only sooth a face ably seared by struggles
to make sense of why colors fade in the sun.

I, too, am in search of color
a shade of tan, perhaps
takes me to those beaches the Beach Boys promised us
just a stroll, a stroke away.

To have done something noble after all
to have strode across the land like Chomsky
reminding us of our imperial designs
colored maps splashed with perilous reds and Libertine golds
all lies to keep us lined up at the malls or on tours of island shores.

We go swimming, others go to jail with no bail
no set release, no charges
the Secret Police won't bother us shopping for an SPF factor 15
or a New Shade for our eyes that don't see the mess
we've made with our indifferent attention to detail.

We have little shame for our wham bam set up for our retirements
where we shall dress in purple and do what we want
we are perfect after all, we can fly.

I, too, am in search of color
a shade of tan perhaps
takes me to those beaches
where time is a lesser god
and all that the Beach Boys promised us
Is a stroll away
Warm seas that never renege on perfect waves.

The Last Page

Roses invite an embrace behind them
the sun filtering through the bamboo
reminds us the weekend was
full of botched chances to rewrite
here, now, on Monday morning
we have time to pause only because
the traffic jam dictates notes on the flowers
lining our shortcuts to old age
and pension plans where we dotter
out to meet with roses who invite us
to embrace now, here finally
Monday morning on the road to work.

Ice

God decided to sit out the century.
After all, the last one dragged even god
around on the Ice Age
it surely was full of cold:
shivering, fearful scenes, phantasmagoria
still, pucks flew into nets, we cheered something to celebrate
surviving holiday games
kids with missing front teeth, incisors
able to walk away after hanging up
razor-sharp blades that cut through the flesh
of the opponents
well, fair enough, everyone expects that in competition
      to win, you cut, tough.
For all of us on the sidelines who never served
or serviced a war on ice or
      Sand or
      Seas
by god, though, we saw our sons skate
through every wimp, every wisp of doubt
those brilliant colors and brand-new sticks
swishing up the slush
god, it can't even end, this– the roundups
the distant chatter, the screams and yells
god shaking hands with another vicious player
in the penalty box, rewards for our diligence pays off
in the final score
then, the lights go out in the arena.
Game over, we can return home now
to hollow glows of glory our victory
is the only thing we truly own
here in my hocked out neighborhood.

Sitting Won't Take Me There

This form, those habits
pieces and shreds of former lives
lie strewn all about the space-time dis
continuum
lines I never learned.
Lines I never told
Smug in my silence
complicit with this arrogant project
of a Universe.

Waiting for Reattachment

Striving for detachment
never meant the retinas.
We need some connections
to make sense of
this round of reality.
So here, in this blurry take
on the New Year's events
renders me shortsighted
even surgery won't restore my
Visions of the Pure Land.

The New Year, opening my eyes –

Ashita ga aru (There's always tomorrow)

No one listens to broken rhythms:
uninflected anything
homogenizes our worldview
to take chances in a foreign tongue
sometimes requires we shout
but our fear lowers our volume.
we whisper responses
to important questions
more worried about
how we sound
      than
      what we say.
Just like our students
we mutter almost incoherently
our mad chatter institutionalizes us
as weird, moronic, inconsequential
when we laugh at others' attempts at our way
      we are laughed at
Every joke I told in my superior, natural English
Echoes back on me as I stand to say something in Japanese.
What was it I was asked?
Sumimasen. Mo sukoshi kangaete itadakimasuka?
To rethink this bursting of the bubble economy.
Itsuka, kitto wakete kureru daro.
(Maybe someday I'll get it.)

The Center Test Poems
(Written while monitoring the national university tests)

I
Cool, grey sniffle
vague wisps of unformed dreams
some sneer, some shake
all bend to the will of the test form
our choices shaved down to a No. 2 pencil.
We're not allowed to sketch
only fill in a pre-ordained circle
time's up.

II
To the Center Test kids:
our responsibility is to help you
fit in sit in this seat, facing forward
we'll tell you all you need to know.

The test begins at ten never be late
don't even consider that
time is something you can't play with
we define reality for you we stand
at the lectern of the status quo.

If you walk out of here
someone will drag you
to the lower depths, lure you away
to an exile of free choices

Too hard to manage.
You're better off here, with us
Safe, warm comatose.

III
Rules of engagement
What we marry, or whom or even why
the choices before us sweep a narrow domain
we think our parameters are wide
unlimited when we face off.
Everyone a potential pal until
we soared free into our teens only
to smack into the walls of the world.

We cannot walk freely with whomever
or travel down a rocky road
with one hand on the wheel.

There are wretched traps for the unwary
laid by our fondest sappers –
the great terrorists of the PTA
What online dating service gets up our ess curves?

We peel back layer after layer
of this onion-skin lie
finding that only our tears remain
with no one to calculate their density
or observe their fall.

To the Mad Hatter
(for David W.)

Have you forgotten
our quiet collusions
nights so full of light
we were spotted by the Hubble
mistaken for a quasar?

Running off to Kansas City
with some floozy of a Fabian?
Shooting off in fireworks of fun
Storming the bastions
of questionable authority?
Walls of doubt crumble surely
clay feet, too.
I'm waiting, wherever.

Conner: Go #27

You came into the lineup a little delayed
kicking your way ahead into the hearts
& minds of all around.
Cheering from the sidelines
I can't help admiring the way
you go about it all, casual
somewhat poised in your approach to the basics.
We debate, pontificate, elaborate
                on the various forms of your futures as we note
                    each sigh each cry each smile each turn
              in the road your pram follows the twists & turns.
                  The warp & woof of your life is laid down
                      here holding you, hanging out
                        weaving with you the tapestry
                          of our steadily
                            unfolding
                            family.

Full Moon Night

I should be howling
instead, I'm locked
in my own mortal fears
can't even sketch
a haiku-like sentiment
crushed by hours
of futile waiting
no cure for this pain
this nausea, no exit
signs everywhere.

This Winter Storm

The cutting edge of the new global warming weather
wild. Surely that's true, what with the Amazon
shrinking into skyscraper canyon walls. Warming
they said, rain that can rip off pine needles and thread
rivulets into the coarsest city streets.

This winter storm snow here so rare now, a
previewing of the next century's motif. Dry, sere gales
up to no good. Here, it snows a reminder of a cooler
era, when we could all drive those big-fin four on the
floor. So cool, we were all so cool. I remember the day
snowflakes last fell. So long, long ago.

On the Way to the Tea Ceremony
with Murder on my Mind

Lock and load
I come to sit in peace
listen to the *matsu no kaze*, the steam
let off more!
Blow away the last vestiges of *tatemae*
here on the tatami, sipping slowly
waiting for my racing emotions
to be whisked away, a sweet
a close examination of the careful
could slake my blood thirst.
I want to stand in the window
with a moral duty to slaughter anyone
who smirks at my sagging face.
Tearoom, a pseudo serene closet of mortality
no one can come out
still, too me, still, be still
this one last sip
then I'll remount my anger
and see where it takes me.

Old Map

Here, I find again the old map to Ni-chome
& all the women's bars with stars.
The winding, narrow streets
labyrinths for the uninitiated home paths
to those of us who no longer need maps.
No, not to this set of boundaries
I know the borders & edges here &
where I can find attractions & distractions
where this ruled off set of rainbow compromises
lurks in a larger context of city/community.

The maps we own, we pour over for direction
tell the world into just which community
we have built our meanings, hammered out a code
        for our behavior, taken precautions
        for the map's limitations
they can't possibly show the wrinkles of every contour
in our cobblestone identities.

Now I put back that precious map
in the drawer of the rosewood desk my lover left me
the maps that remind me of all my journeys
to my places in the heart.

I Don't Know

what a man is
because I've never
pleased one
wanted one
been one
wanted to become one
needed one
needed to be with one
been seen by one
   so
   what &
   me
   a woman, or at least
   something
other
   than a
   Man hunter
      hater
      lover
& you?
I need no more of you
   than
   your shadow is willing
   to show me.

Elder Fall

I was trying to dig my heels into the sands of time
when I tripped & fell back into the aches & pains of being.
Before I was a Leo I was a brownie, both IDs chosen
by Someone Other, not me, never graduating
to a Virgo say, or a Girl Scout.
I hang around on Humbug hillsides
in love with the Milky Way.
My elder alder, too, tripped and fell, crossed the creek
creating a hardwood bridge
to and from new possibilities for metaphor.
Without that giant, mossy giver of shade
the Steelhead packed up, moved downstream
Humbug Creek too hot to handle here
now open, more Milky Way to see.
My companion for nearly thirty years shady, sighing
part & parcel of my main stem will now warm Winter friends.
Ashes to ashes, alders to Alders
We await our seedling renewal.

Dialing for Deities

Call up God and whattya get?
Either a busy signal or an answer machine with no answers
just "Hello, God's not in right now but your call
is important to us. So if this is about past sins, press one ..."
God never calls back, even the Holy Ghost
who hangs out in my higher moments
doesn't spell out anything anymore on the Ouija board
can you tell me why or how this hissy fit
of a universe keeps us in agreement?
So much suffering is not what we'd have in mind.

War crimes tribunals never reach up the ladder
to whatever dirty deity slapped this together
rush order, probably in seven days
with no more thought than a casual "Let there be light."

Condemn you we will
or take sides with the atheists
who at least believe in living.

Amaterasu, Yahweh, Isis, money
the deities of our choice have unlisted numbers
we could sue in some cosmic court
or open their doors and drag them down
to the lower depths
to hell with the lot of 'em.

In the Window

You admired my stained glass. In the window of my office, catching the weak winter sun. Casting crimson dancers on the wall, near where we were discussing your MA proposal.

"Bleeding Cunt" is the title of the glass. Look here, these drops of red, lips of lacy shells. Embedded, blending into the design...

"Oh, how pornographic!" Your comment shows me that perhaps it is better to not know learning what or who something is called. Leads us down grooves and ruts in the memories of our moral education, so we lose sight as soon as we see we were sitting sipping rose hip tea, talking of Rhys and the Wide Sargasso Sea, safe.

How Many?

500 X 500
Not just 500 dead
Everyone around them took a hit;
Moms, dads, high school friends,
500 now is it?
The others, the ones who came to pray in mosques
Children of antique alleys
Playing in the ruins of all our ambitions
Women washing out the damned spots
Mechanic called in to fix an angry tank
Merchants chatting among the hopeful in line
Trying to find out where everyone goes after
They're thrown on the trucks:
Headquarters, surely
Not
Some whole in the wall
Hell hole of our outsourced torture
Surely no goose-stepping again, are we?
So many others:
The ones who question
The ones who can give no answers
Marchers, mothers
The bombed out and the burned out
The ones who escape, or try to escape or
Think about escaping this
New world terror stalking our streets,
Footpaths and fastracks
We've no place to hide
Our world in our hands.

Why Should I Feel Depressed Sitting in a Laundromat

At 5:30, dinnertime with detergents scrubbing my soul
      (Used to imagine my soul was a tiny sewing machine
in back of my navel &
      grace was pure, white grease I would rub into it with
      a few magic indulgences whispered by a priest in a
      long black dress, sterile clean)
Sweat counts for nothing here except scorn.

Outside, the city wheezes & chokes on its phlegm
sometimes, I'm ready to believe they served the Holy
Ghost under glass & now there's only one God
sometimes, people shuffle past the misty window
helpless it seems to stop themselves from soaking
into the sidewalk alone maybe for now unable
to read the patterns on the river or hear
the warnings quaking from deep in my heart.

Right on the edge, I feel a razor slicing open the fabric
of what is to be people's hatred & anger flushing
out landlords, cowering behind a long black dress.
Scour away the tear stains from our beds
voices from other rooms open doors & hesitantly
take each other's hands, together we chase
the yellow fog back to the sea & tear down
smokestacks aimlessly pushing around the sky.

Ripping Off Good Times

Everyone needs shadow times
spasms only a stranger could soothe.

They even chained the stars
spring winds are full of sirens so loud
we can't shout our love for the heroes
falling asleep at the bar.

We've seen the Holy Ghost stashed in lard cans
behind the concession at the Drive Inn
where search & destroy from Mission Control
is sold over the counter.

If human flesh burns with a fragrant
oriental tang, make it into tea
& i will drink it with a pinch of spice.

Come summer we should blow up
our barbed-wire dreams
grab the mud from our boot heels &
smear the walls with slogans of our Esteem.

Rip off our silk gags & we will speak to the sun.

Then we can meet together in quiet dawn
chop down all our crosses, hop over to the shady
side of the snack bar & roll the moon
for every second chance its got.

I Did Not Mean To

Take away your pride by
Feeding you grounds for
Codeine with glass
Pain, I suppose, can teach a lot but
When someone really doesn't need a hard lesson
The whole world notices my sin by your limp.
They filed down your kneecaps
Making a point of my sins &
You'll never genuflect to
Anyone again.
Now you know that
Social workers
Wear stacked heels to
Jack themselves up so they can
Face the people.
I, on the other hand,
Creep
In the hollow regions of my eyes
Hoping today you won't notice the
Shadows of my
Temper.
I owe the world a debt for
My anger
Not because I had no reason but
Because
I never learned in time
Strength means
Countering with love
Our memories
Stretching across the future.
Somehow you understood
Why &
Never demanded an
Explanation.

Dick Wrap

A subspecies of bats
Discovered kinky sex six thousand years ago
Deep down, waggling around dark caves
the oversized dicks substitute for arms
"Oh, cuddle me babe, its damp and cold in here.
Evolve with me a moment
Why, we ask, sonic furry freaks dwelling in caves
Get the long end of the stick
(and no penetration??) honey you got no imagination.
the comfort zone for sex expands
A stroke me moment for males:
It's not the banging but the boa wrap around that
Shows us the way to hang it up, lay back and have some
Synced, kinked sonic fun outta the sun.
The takeaway might be:
You get more bang for your buck by cuddling;
(but that's just bats!)

Narita to Me

Wild walk through the
Xenophobic maze of
Misapprehensions
Ironed out, flatlined any hope of
Remaining off the grid(dle)
Fone, forced into my dinosaur
Hands to track where I would be
Me
Alone in the neighborhood of
Impatience;
How do you dial up some fun, hon?
Text try:
No I don't have any symptoms you motherfuckers
Masked, all, waiting for results
Two besties scrape me off the exit door of the airport and
Drive me mad(ly) to bed
This city, Kiyose,
Shut up, closed down,
Musing on malaise…
Old crumbs on the floor
Feeding the Kafka cockroach
Crawling across my kitchen, but mine
Refugee from America macho misogyny
I just want to be free
In Kiyose shi
I want to be free
Free,
Me

Five Ways Out
(for Karen, Mark, Conner, Samantha, Mia)

Come sing me
the soft wind &
let me beat
the drum slowly
for your light step.
My Rhubarb wine
hints of Spring &
rituals of the newborn
bubble gum anarchists
search your attics
for silver dreams
if the sun rises
wake me with a shout

Biography

Co-founder of *Tokyo Poetry Journal*, Barbara splits her time
between her cabin in the hills of Oregon and her house in
Kiyose, at the edge of Tokyo. She lives her life in longhand,
and stargazes from fields both in Oregon and Kiyose.
Retired, she is still in touch with her students of Daito Bunka
University, where she is a Professor Emeritus. Her poetry
has appeared in *The Spirit that Moves Us*, *Printed Matter*, *The
Applegater* newspaper, *Common Woman*, *Poet and Critic*, *Koe*,
Maize, *New Yarn*, and several anthologies. As she holds a 7th
dan in Aikido, she occasionally teaches here and there.